Spring

Julie Murray

Abdo
SEASONS
Kids

abdopublishing.com

Published by Abdo Kids, a division of ABDO, PO Box 398166, Minneapolis, Minnesota 55439.
Copyright © 2016 by Abdo Consulting Group, Inc. International copyrights reserved in all countries.
No part of this book may be reproduced in any form without written permission from the publisher.

Printed in the United States of America, North Mankato, Minnesota.

052015

092015

Photo Credits: iStock, Shutterstock

Production Contributors: Teddy Borth, Jennie Forsberg, Grace Hansen

Design Contributors: Candice Keimig, Dorothy Toth

Library of Congress Control Number: 2014958733

Cataloging-in-Publication Data

Murray, Julie.

 Spring / Julie Murray.

   p. cm. -- (Seasons)

ISBN 978-1-62970-920-8

Includes index.

1. Spring--Juvenile literature. 2. Seasons--Juvenile literature.   I. Title.

508.2--dc23

                    2014958733

Table of Contents

Spring

Spring is one of the
four seasons.

Spring

Summer

Winter

Fall

5

The sun feels warmer in Spring.

The days get longer.

Plants begin to grow.

Flowers **bloom**.

8

Birds build **nests**.

They lay their eggs.

Many baby animals are born.

The **piglets** are so cute!

Farmers plant **crops**.

The corn grows fast.

14

It can be windy.

Jimmy flies a kite.

It often rains. Grace likes
to jump in puddles.

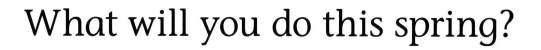

What will you do this spring?

Spring Fun

feed ducks

jump in puddles

fly a kite

plant flowers

Glossary

bloom
when a flower opens from a bud.

nest
a home made by a bird for laying eggs and keeping its babies safe.

crop
a plant that is grown as food, like grain, fruit, or vegetable.

piglet
a baby pig.

Index

abdokids.com

Use this code to log on to abdokids.com and access crafts, games, videos, and more!

Abdo Kids Code:
SSK9208